Our Soppy love Story

A Journal About Us

Our Soppy love Story

philippa Rice

Andrews McMeel
PUBLISHING®

For Luke

How to Use This Book

This is a guided journal for two people to complete.

It's all about documenting your relationship, your feelings,
and your lives together.

You can fill it in in order,
or skip ahead and complete any page you feel like.

You can write or draw your answers. If you both want
to complete the same page, use different colored pens.

Together...

Individually...

Keep this book around

and fill it in every once in a while.

My idea is that by documenting the small moments in our lives, we can appreciate them more.

I hope that in this book you can capture a time in your life, and in the future,

read it back and remember

how it all felt.

Me & you

Portrait (or photo):

Names:

Our Story

How we met:

About Us

Full names:

Birthdays:

Star signs:

Address:

What do we do?

Living arrangement:

Who we are RIGHT NOW

Today's date:

Current ages:

Nicknames / Pet names:

Current hairstyles:

What are our lives like?

Right Now

mood:

daydreaming about:

I appreciate:

trying not to
think about:

This page filled in by: [   ]

date:

Me, right now:

feeling ...

Memorable Times

Occasions in our relationship so far...

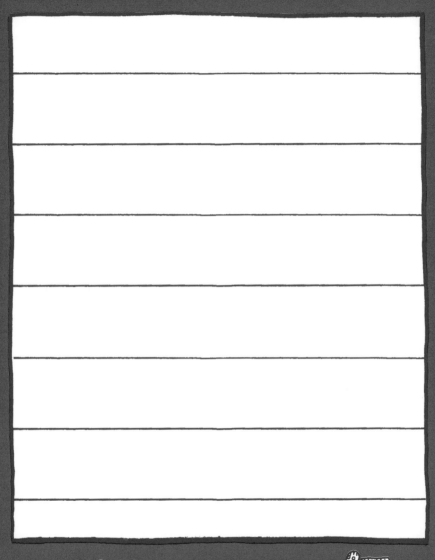

what I like about you

1 _____

2 _____

3 _____

4 _____

5 _____

This page filled in by: [   ] About: [   ]

6 _____

7 _____

8 _____

9 _____

10 _____

Our Favorite Books

Today

Something we did...

today was...

- [ ] sweet
- [ ] fun
- [ ] relaxed
- [ ] dull
- [ ] different
- [ ] productive
- [ ] comfortable
- [ ] happy
- [ ] gloomy

- [ ] stressful
- [ ] pleasant
- [ ] hard
- [ ] exciting
- [ ] confusing
- [ ] amazing
- [ ] _____
- [ ] _____
- [ ] _____

Would you Rather...

Never read a book again	☐	☐	Never eat a dessert again
Be able to talk to animals	☐	☐	Be able to read minds (human minds)
Be invisible	☐	☐	Be the only person who's not invisible
Eat a spider	☐	☐	Kiss a pig
Have to wear high heels always	☐	☐	Have to wear a top hat always

Your own "would you rather" questions ...

written by:

answered by:

☐ ☐

☐ ☐

☐ ☐

☐ ☐

☐ ☐

About Me

Things that always make me smile :

_____

_____

_____

_____

_____

_____

My ideal day:

_____

_____

_____

_____

_____

_____

Ideas

Things to do today

Bake bread together

Light a bunch of candles

Watch cute puppy videos

Go for a walk

Read a comic book together

Wrestle

Talk about your dreams

Tidy the cupboards

Do a face mask

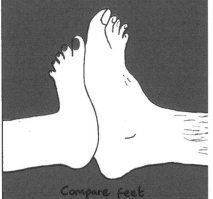

Invent a new card game

Compare feet

Right Now

date:

filled in by:

I can hear:

I can see:

I can smell:

I feel...

Hugs

Vote for your favorites

Yes No
☐ ☐   Rating ♡ ♡ ♡ ♡ ♡

Yes No
☐ ☐   Rating ♡ ♡ ♡ ♡ ♡

Yes No
☐ ☐   Rating ♡ ♡ ♡ ♡ ♡

Yes No
☐ ☐   Rating ♡♡♡♡♡

Yes No
☐ ☐   Rating ♡♡♡♡♡

Yes No
☐ ☐   Rating ♡♡♡♡♡

Yes No
☐ ☐   Rating ♡♡♡♡♡

Yes No
☐ ☐   Rating ♡ ♡ ♡ ♡ ♡

draw some more...

Yes No
☐ ☐   Rating ♡ ♡ ♡ ♡ ♡

Yes No
☐ ☐   Rating ♡ ♡ ♡ ♡ ♡

Yes No
☐ ☐   Rating ♡ ♡ ♡ ♡ ♡

Yes No

☐ ☐   Rating ♡ ♡ ♡ ♡ ♡   Yes No

☐ ☐   Rating ♡ ♡ ♡ ♡ ♡

Yes No

☐ ☐   Rating ♡ ♡ ♡ ♡ ♡   Yes No

☐ ☐   Rating ♡ ♡ ♡ ♡ ♡

Need to Know

Favorite flowers

Colors/shades

Fabric/texture

fruit

Genre (Films/TV)

Genre (books)

Season

Sandwich

Weather

Today

date:

today we did...

Today, my face was like:

Because:

Because:

Because:

Because:

Questions

I: [   ]

Would Like to Ask

You: [   ]

?

Question: _____

Answer:

?

Question: _____

Answer:

?

Question: _____

Answer:

Question: _____ ?

Answer:

Question: _____ ?

Answer:

Question: _____ ?

Answer:

Question: _____ ?

Answer:

About Us

phrases / words / lines we often use:

_____

_____

_____

_____

_____

_____

what are we good at as a team?

_____

_____

_____

_____

_____

Which Is Best?

filled in by: [   ]

Outdoors ☐	☐ Indoors	
The sun ☐	☐ The Moon	
Fruit ☐	☐ Vegetables	
Books ☐	☐ Movies	
Fantasy ☐	☐ Reality	
Sweet ☐	☐ Savory	

Warm ☐ ☐ Cool

Mountains ☐ ☐ The sea

Bright colors ☐ ☐ Classy neutrals

Dancing ☐ ☐ Singing

Tea ☐ ☐ Coffee

Wild times ☐ ☐ Cozy times

phone call ☐ ☐ Texting

Right Now

My outfit:

what's on my mind:

Our favorite
BReakFasts

Our Favorite Lunches

_____

_____

_____

_____

_____

our favorite
Desserts

_____

_____

_____

_____

_____

About [you: _____]
by [me: _____]

How would you describe their personality?

_____

_____

_____

What do you think is their weakness?

_____

_____

_____

What is their strength?

_____

_____

_____

_____

What is the kindest thing they've ever done for you?

_____

_____

_____

This page filled in by: [ ]

date:

Something that happened...

Today I am...

- ☐ Strong
- ☐ Bored
- ☐ Tired
- ☐ Energized
- ☐ Amazing
- ☐ Up and down
- ☐ Comfortable
- ☐ Weak
- ☐ Sassy

- ☐ Happy
- ☐ Productive
- ☐ Relaxed
- ☐ Angry
- ☐ Annoying
- ☐ Motivated
- ☐ _____
- ☐ _____
- ☐ _____

Something we would like more of:

And something we would like less of:

About Us

Our traditions:

_____

_____

_____

_____

_____

_____

A typical day in the life of us...

"Secret" wish list of gifts I'd be happy to receive any time:

Filled in by:

Right Now

The environment surrounding me:

filled in by: ▮▮▮▮▮

Yes   No

	Yes	No
Content	☐	☐
Tired	☐	☐
Sensitive	☐	☐
Positive	☐	☐
Warm	☐	☐
Fresh	☐	☐
Relaxed	☐	☐
Hungry	☐	☐
Thirsty	☐	☐
Nervous	☐	☐
Anxious	☐	☐
Settled	☐	☐
Inspired	☐	☐

date: ⬭   time: ⬭

What is important to you?

choose three and circle them.

Knowledge   Strength

            Power

Security   Style

            Fun

Weirdness   Spirituality

            Work

Creativity   Excitement

Art

Filled in by: [＿＿＿＿＿＿＿]

Humor

Sports

Space

Opportunities

Animals

Food

Self-expression

Empathy

Passion

Something else?

Dreams

◯

Filled in by: ▭ Date: ▭

IMPORTANT!

♥ If I become a zombie, please...

1. Kill me ☐   2. Leave me alone ☐   3. Allow me to bite you ☐

4. keep me contained somewhere safe ☐   5. Other ▭

♥ Do I want my brain to be brought back to life in the form of a robot/android/computer?

Yes ☐   No ☐   Other ▭

♥ Am I interested in becoming immortal?   Yes ☐ No ☐

What if it meant becoming a vampire?   Yes ☐ No ☐

Even if it's a "good" Vampire?   Yes ☐ No ☐

♥ If you get caught up in some weird crime thing, please:

1. Tell me/ get me involved ☐   2. keep me out of it ☐

3. other ▭

Memories

A vacation or trip we've been on together...

filled in by: [ ]

Today

This page filled in by: [ ]

date:

Something we did...

today was...

- [ ] sweet
- [ ] fun
- [ ] relaxed
- [ ] dull
- [ ] different
- [ ] productive
- [ ] comfortable
- [ ] happy
- [ ] gloomy

- [ ] stressful
- [ ] pleasant
- [ ] hard
- [ ] exciting
- [ ] confusing
- [ ] amazing
- [ ]
- [ ]
- [ ]

ideas for staying in:

_____

_____

_____

_____

_____

_____

places we could visit together:

_____

_____

_____

_____

_____

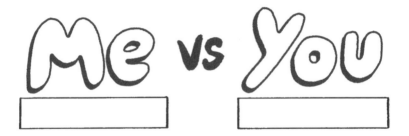

Me vs You

which one of us is...

	Me	You
The most ticklish	☐	☐
The tidiest	☐	☐
The warmest	☐	☐
The cleverest	☐	☐
The strongest	☐	☐
The silliest	☐	☐
The most optimistic	☐	☐
The calmest	☐	☐
The most sophisticated	☐	☐

The best cook | Me ☐ | You ☐

The most in charge | Me ☐ | You ☐

The most organized | Me ☐ | You ☐

The clumsiest | Me ☐ | You ☐

The most fit | Me ☐ | You ☐

The sleepiest | Me ☐ | You ☐

The most grumpy | Me ☐ | You ☐

The most talkative | Me ☐ | You ☐

The most practical | Me ☐ | You ☐

The most competitive | Me ☐ | You ☐

The bravest | Me ☐ | You ☐

The best singer | Me ☐ | You ☐

Portraits of

Portrait of: _____ by: _____

Each Other

Portrait of: _____ by: _____

Right Now

daydreaming about:

mood:

trying not to
think about:

I appreciate:

This page filled in by: [　　　　] date:

Me, right now:

feeling ...

Surprises

Filled in by: _____

Do you like surprises? Yes ☐ No ☐

What <u>kind</u> of surprises do you think you'd appreciate?

_____

_____

_____

_____

_____

_____

_____

You need to know,
I don't like surprises

A surprise takes away
the joy of looking forward
to something

So... If you're planning an
elaborate surprise gift for me,
(maybe it's a vacation?) you can
tell me now

Well... I'm not but I'll bear that
in mind

About Me

filled in by:

What interests me?

_____

_____

_____

_____

_____

_____

what bores me?

_____

_____

_____

_____

_____

what makes you cry?

What cheers you up?

This page filled in by:

Today

date:

One thing we did...

Rating for today: ★ ★ ★ ★ ★

Another thing...

Ideas

Things to do today

Swap clothes

Research Something

Thumb war

Stare out of the window

Draw a tattoo

Paint Something

Plant Something

Mail Something

Picnic

Do a yoga Video

Watch a movie

About our extended family:

Our Favorite Movies

_____

_____

_____

_____

_____

_____

_____

_____

_____

Do you think we should turn the heat on?

Right Now

Mood:

My current look:

your current look:

mood:

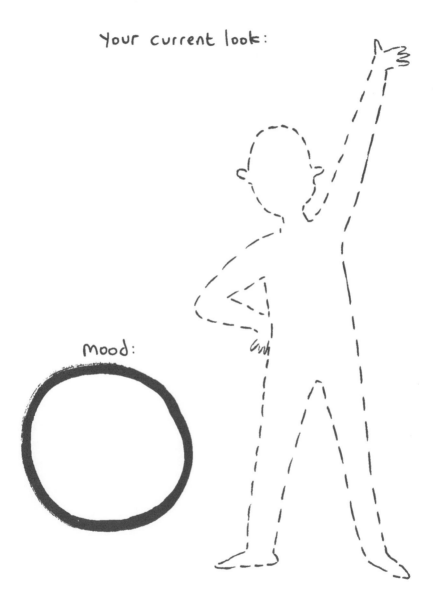

What to have for dinner...

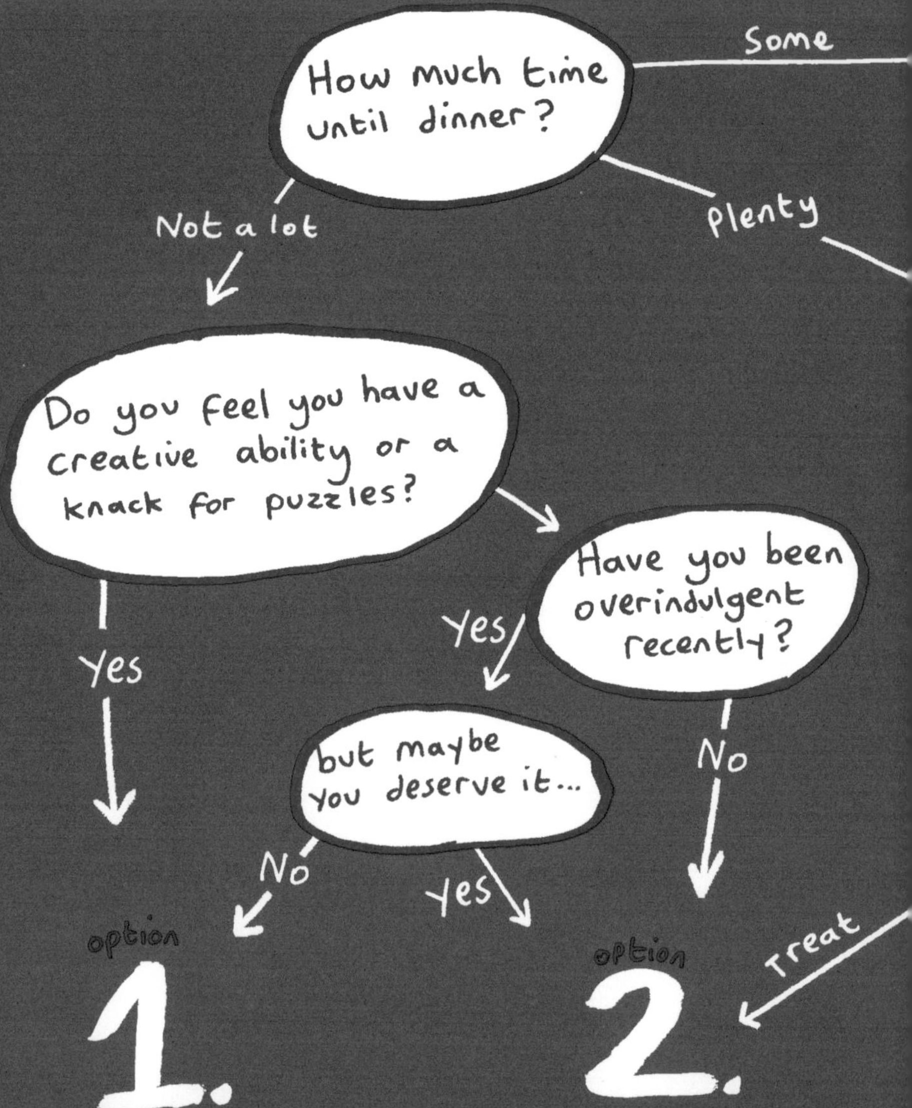

Turn the page to see the results...

What's the weather like?

Cold

Warm

Are you feeling bold, strong, and ready for anything?

Yes

Nope

Right now, which animal do you feel an affinity with? Hedgehog or falcon?

Would you prefer a hug or a treat?

Hedgehog

Falcon

Hug

option 3.

option 4.

1 Use whatever you have in the fridge

Spaghetti with garlic oil and olives? Breakfast for dinner? Something from the freezer?

2 Take-out!

Order in whatever you want. You deserve it!

3 Comfort food

Lasagna, casserole, soup, and crusty bread.

4 Fancy new recipe

Look up a recipe, go out and buy ingredients, try something new!

About [you: ___]
by [me: ___]

which famous people do they look like?

_____

_____

_____

_____

_____

_____

In what ways have they affected, changed, or influenced you?

_____

_____

_____

_____

_____

_____

Today

This page filled in by:

date:

Something we did...

today was...

- [ ] sweet
- [ ] fun
- [ ] relaxed
- [ ] dull
- [ ] different
- [ ] productive
- [ ] comfortable
- [ ] happy
- [ ] gloomy

- [ ] stressful
- [ ] pleasant
- [ ] hard
- [ ] exciting
- [ ] confusing
- [ ] amazing
- [ ]
- [ ]
- [ ]

Our Sleeping Positions...

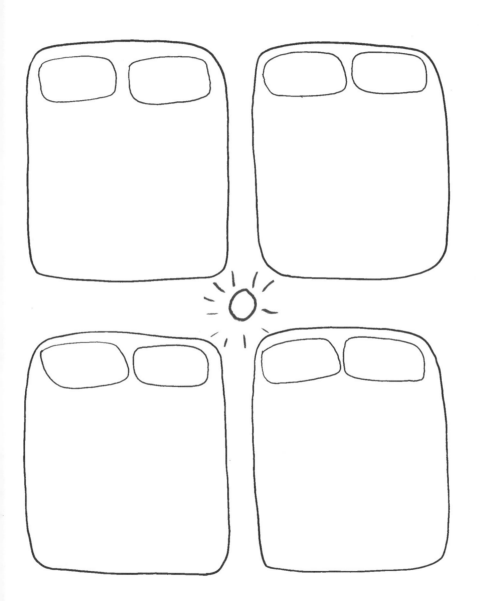

DREAMS

Dreams you've had involving each other...

About Us

How open-minded are we?

_____

_____

_____

_____

_____

_____

What has been our biggest adventure so far?

_____

_____

_____

_____

_____

Right Now

Current agenda / goals :

What I'm doing now:

what I'll do next:

My face:

Hugs

Vote for your
Favorites

Yes No ☐ ☐ Rating ♡ ♡ ♡ ♡ ♡

Yes No ☐ ☐ Rating ♡ ♡ ♡ ♡ ♡

Yes No ☐ ☐ Rating ♡ ♡ ♡ ♡ ♡

Rating ♡♡♡♡♡

Rating ♡♡♡♡♡

Rating ♡♡♡♡♡

Rating ♡♡♡♡♡

Yes No Rating ♡♡♡♡♡

Yes No Rating ♡♡♡♡♡

Yes No Rating ♡♡♡♡♡

Yes No Rating ♡♡♡♡♡

Yes No

☐ ☐ Rating ♡ ♡ ♡ ♡ ♡

Yes No

☐ ☐ Rating ♡ ♡ ♡ ♡ ♡

Yes No

☐ ☐ Rating ♡ ♡ ♡ ♡ ♡

Yes No

☐ ☐ Rating ♡ ♡ ♡ ♡ ♡

Some of Our Favorite People

This page filled in by: _____

Today

date:

Something that happened...

Mood

_____

The absolute pits   Sparkling zest for life

Style

_____

Dressed in a sack   Perfectly put together

Productivity

_____

I'm still in bed   Blasting through my goals

Personality Test

Complete the drawings any way you like.

1.

2.

3.

4.

5.

6.

Filled in by: [_____]

Describe each picture in one or two adjectives.

1. _____

2. _____

3. _____

4. _____

5. _____

6. _____

See the next page for results!

what you wrote... →

1. Your friends are... _____

Accurate? ☐ Yes ☐ No

2. You like to think of yourself as... _____

Accurate? ☐ Yes ☐ No

3. You would like to be more... _____

Accurate? ☐ Yes ☐ No

4. You don't like situations that are... _____

Accurate? ☐ Yes ☐ No

5. Your relationship is... _____

Accurate? ☐ Yes ☐ No

6. Your dream future is... _____

Accurate? ☐ Yes ☐ No

What Kind of Monsters Scare You?

_____

_____

_____

_____

_____

Real things that scare you...

Right Now

date:

filled in by:

I can hear:

I can see:

I can smell:

I feel...

Drawings of
Our Treasured Possessions

what is it?	what is it?
How/where did you get it?	How/where did you get it?

what is it?	what is it?
How/where did you get it?	How/where did you get it?

what is it?

How/where did you get it?

what is it?

How/where did you get it?

what is it?

How/where did you get it?

what is it?

How/where did you get it?

what is it?

How/where did you get it?

what is it?

How/where did you get it?

what is it?

How/where did you get it?

what is it?

How/where did you get it?

what is it?

How/where did you get it?

what is it?

How/where did you get it?

what is it?

How/where did you get it?

what is it?

How/where did you get it?

Today

This page filled in by: _____

date:

Something that happened...

Today I am...

- ☐ Strong
- ☐ Bored
- ☐ Tired
- ☐ Energized
- ☐ Amazing
- ☐ Up and down
- ☐ Comfortable
- ☐ Weak
- ☐ Sassy

- ☐ Happy
- ☐ Productive
- ☐ Relaxed
- ☐ Angry
- ☐ Annoying
- ☐ Motivated
- ☐ _____
- ☐ _____
- ☐ _____

About Me

What do I do to calm down and relax?

_____

_____

_____

_____

_____

_____

What energizes me and wakes me up?

_____

_____

_____

_____

_____

Draw a celebrity and the other person has to guess who it is.

clue:

guess:

Correct?

yes   no

Our Favorite Games

Right Now

my outfit:

what's on my mind:

Our Favorite Songs

How clean and tidy is our home today?

Sludge pit   It'll do   Sparkling

Maybe it's too clean? ☐

Task:
_____

Who usually does it ?

Task:
_____

Who usually does it ?

Task:
_____

Who usually does it ?

Task:
_____

Who usually does it ?

Housework

Housework strategy:

Task:
_____

Who usually does it?

Task:
_____

Who usually does it?

Task:
_____

Who usually does it?

Task:
_____

Who usually does it?

What is our home like?

Today

This page filled in by: ☐

date: ◯

today we did...

Today, my face was like:

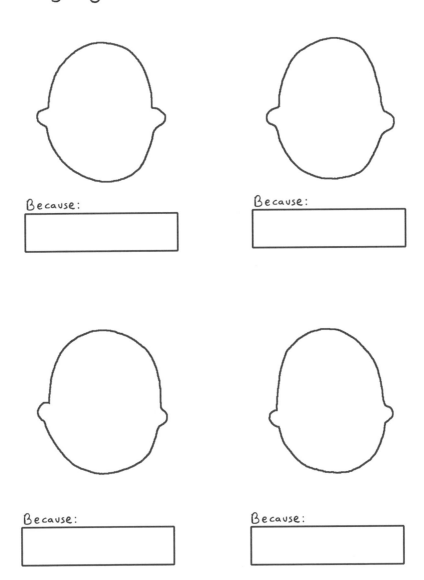

Because:

Because:

Because:

Because:

About Us

Things we disagree on:

_____

_____

_____

_____

_____

_____

Things we agree on:

_____

_____

_____

_____

_____

_____

Test
your psychic abilities

Psychically project an animal and the other person tries to read your mind.

the animal:

First try:

_____

second guess:

_____

third:

_____

are you psychic?

☐ yes ☐ no ☐ maybe

what is it like where we live?

Right Now

mood:

daydreaming about:

I appreciate:

trying not to
think about:

This page filled in by: _____ date:

Me, right now:

feeling...

What's on the cards?

Choose a DVD or book at random.

Find the seventh number in the bar code.

Match the number to one of the cards on the right. →

Which card was it:

How might that relate to your future?

Confession Time

filled in by:

Here's what I REALLY thought when I first met you...

Here's something I only do when you're not around...

This is my secret regret...

This is what i'm secretly proud of...

Anything else you want to confess?

A stressful time for us...

filled in by: [ ]

HATE LIST

The _worst_ things ↓

Today

date:

Something that happened...

mood

The absolute pits ——————————— Sparkling zest for life

Style

Dressed in a sack ——————————— Perfectly put together

Productivity

I'm still in bed ——————————— Blasting through my goals

What gets you out of bed in the morning?

what do you think about as you go to sleep?

Filled in by: [   ]

One thing we'd like to add to our life

Questions
Would Like to Ask

I: [   ]

You: [   ]

?

Question: _____

Answer:

?

Question: _____

Answer:

?

Question: _____

Answer:

Question: _____ ?

Answer:

Question: _____ ?

Answer:

Question: _____ ?

Answer:

Question: _____ ?

Answer:

Right Now

date:

filled in by:

Current agenda / goals :

What I'm doing now:

what I'll do next:

My face:

Drawings of Our favorite

Item:

Memories associated with it?

Item:

Memories associated with it?

Item:

Memories associated with it?

Item:

Memories associated with it?

Items of Clothing

(and accessories)

Item:

Memories associated with it?

Item:

Memories associated with it?

Item:

Memories associated with it?

Item:

Memories associated with it?

Magical Pet

Draw half of an animal each to create your magical pet.

Name:

First half of each of your first names
plus the second half of each of your surnames

Have you ever...

Felt the presence of a ghost?

Had a crush on a cartoon character?

Kissed an animal on the lips?

Stayed awake all night?

Eaten food that you
dropped on the floor?

Served food that you dropped
on the floor to another person?

filled in by: _____

Thrown an unwanted gift in the trash?   Yes ☐ No ☐

Lied about your age?   Yes ☐ No ☐

Eaten alone in a restaurant?   Yes ☐ No ☐

Had a dream that came true?   Yes ☐ No ☐

Gone shopping for groceries
and eaten some on the way home?   Yes ☐ No ☐

Told a lie in this book?   Yes ☐ No ☐

This page filled in by: [_____]

Today

date:

Something we did...

Today I am...

- [ ] Strong
- [ ] Bored
- [ ] Tired
- [ ] Energized
- [ ] Amazing
- [ ] Up and down
- [ ] Comfortable
- [ ] Weak
- [ ] Sassy

- [ ] Happy
- [ ] Productive
- [ ] Relaxed
- [ ] Angry
- [ ] Annoying
- [ ] Motivated
- [ ] _____
- [ ] _____
- [ ] _____

This is what I think is good
advice for relationships:

by: ⬚

what I like about you

1 _____

2 _____

3 _____

4 _____

5 _____

This page filled in by: [　　　　　] About : [　　　　　]

6 _____

7 _____

8 _____

9 _____

10 _____

About Us

Updates/changes since we started this book: